SELIMA HILL

Bunny

BLOODAXE BOOKS

Copyright © Selima Hill 2001

ISBN: 1 85224 507 7

First published 2001 by
Bloodaxe Books Ltd,
Highgreen,
Tarset,
Northumberland NE48 1RP.

Second impression 2002

Printed in Great Britain by
Cromwell Press Ltd, Trowbridge, Wiltshire.

CONTENTS

7	Little Dogs	44	Scarf
8	Fun	45	Home
9	Shoes	46	Doorway
10	Hens	47	Terrace Gardens
11	Tulips	48	Boiled Sweets
12	Pyjama-case	49	Shimmering Lakes
13	Angel-Top	50	Sapphire
14	Ponyskin	51	Taffeta
15	Passion-Fruit	52	Milk
16	Pool	53	Songbirds
17	House	54	Shame
18	PRAWNS DE JO	55	Dawn
20	Mussels	56	Wristwatch
21	Cashmere	57	Aunt Lou's Last Summer
22	Lips	58	Help
23	Egg	59	Rain
24	Plums	60	Running
25	Vaseline	61	River
26	Sheets	62	Blancmange
27	Chicken	63	Angora
28	Jacket	64	Budgie
29	Bedding	65	Doctor
30	Bolero	66	How
31	Everything	68	Mercy
32	Roses	69	Hairbrush
33	Ultramarine	70	Arm
34	Larches	71	Lobster
35	Baby	72	A Thousand Swifts
36	Moon	73	Galloping Alopecia
37	Stars	74	Nothing
38	Balaclava	75	An Angel with Large Hands
39	Snakes	76	Colonnades
40	Sheep	77	Motes
41	Suitcase	78	The Room
42	Cows	79	Sky
43	Bulls	80	Blue

ACKNOWLEDGEMENTS

Acknowledgements are due to the editors of the following publications in which some of these poems first appeared: *Bulletin of the Royal College of Psychiatry, Daily Express, Flora Poetica* (Chatto, 2001), *The Independent, The Lancet, Mind the Gap* (New York), Poetry International programme, *Pink Ribbon, Poetry Ireland, Poetry Review, The Rialto, Second Light* (Enitharmon Press, 2000), *Stand, Time's Tidings* (Anvil Press Poetry, 1999) and *Times Educational Supplement*.

'The Room' was a runner-up in the Arvon/*Observer* International Poetry Competition and was published in the competition anthology. 'How' was commissioned by the Museum of London for the London Festival. 'An Angel with Large Hands' was originally written as part of an Opera Lab commission, while 'Hairbrush' was first recorded by Peter Bevan for Shaftesbury Films. 'PRAWNS DE JO' and 'The Room' were included on the cassette tape *The Poetry Quartets: 2* (The British Council/Bloodaxe Books, 1998).

I am indebted to Ben and Billy Taylor of Double Helix for the use of their title *Shimmering Lakes*. I would also like to thank the present occupier of the house where most of this story takes place for their kind response to a letter from a perfect stranger.

I would like to dedicate this book to two hard-working people who, without really knowing what was happening, seem to have changed my life, and I am very grateful to them: Sister Winniki, my Estonian nurse, and Bent Sørensen, composer, from Denmark.

Little Dogs

She feels so proud to be so under-nourished
and not to have her aunts all turning up

with little dogs on leads, and tartan rugs;
she feels so proud to be alone at home

like someone in a hangar after midnight
entrusted with the mothering of jets.

Fun

She wanted fun.
What she gets is tartan,

the classics, and a little wholesome food;
what she gets is toothpaste,

and the lodger,
who thanks You for inventing thighs, O Lord.

Shoes

A row of shoes,
a man in silk pyjamas,

unsettle,
like a necklace dipped in dust,

an absent father,
and the father's house.

Hens

The fridge is full of hens.
It's Friday night.

Her only comfort is the word *vanilla*.
She says it again and again till she falls asleep

She's the only child on earth
who's not allowed ice-cream.

Tulips

What the smell of the smell of her girlfriend's boyfriend's
        jumper
does to her dreams

is nobody's business but hers,
nor the smell of the lodger

going upstairs with his tulips
and passing her by on her bed like a still-born lamb.

Pyjama-case

A small pyjama-case was all she wanted
but what she gets is this enormous house

where nobody touches
and even the beds are cold

and a silver spoon is the size of a cold lily
and the lodger is wearing a floor-length satin dressing-gown

and the bathroom is panelled with mirrors like flattened eyes
in one of which he watches as she pouts

while posing on the rim of the bath
in a bra with cups the size of elastic pudding-basins.

Angel-Top

She feels lovely
in her Angel-Top

and Slipper-Sox
with pimples like rare fruit

that sparkle in the sky
where Cassiopeia

leaning from her sapphire roost
is calling.

Ponyskin

Sedated and grubby like snow
that's falling apart,

she shouldn't be doing this here
when the lights are out

and the blue of the hall
is the black of a swollen river

and there's somebody padding around in his ponyskin slippers
wondering what on earth is going on.

Passion-Fruit

The passion-fruit resembles
coloured bruises

rolled
into a ball you can suck.

Pool

Athletic and chaste,
she plunges into the pool,

leaving the lodger
alone in the house with the dust

and nothing to shine on or do,
like a chandelier.

House

She sleeps in late
as if the house were hers

but it is his.
She should have been more careful.

She should have been attentive
to his timing.

The fact that she was wrong
and he was right.

PRAWNS DE JO

Because she was wrong,
because it was all her fault right from the beginning,
because she was ashamed of even thinking about it,
and should never have been his daughter in the first place;
because she was ugly
and he was magnificent
and she was the scum of the earth,
it must never be mentioned:
the unforgettable smell of the singeing baby,
the unforgettable sight of billowing curtains like brides,
the cot,
the charred muslin,
the endless procession of leggy inquisitive flies,
the orange buzz of the electric fire,
and how she'd sit for hours squeezing oranges,
and how she'd sit and fan the flies away,
and hurry down the streets with aching breasts
to part the veil of flies to please the doctors,
the orange ash, the orange carrot-juice,
are never to be mentioned. In that case
what is she to do with the head
that has to be oiled and covered and never mentioned,
as crisp as the colour of violets sprinkled with salt
that grow in the dark
to within half an inch of her brain,
as the colour of prawns sprinkled with salt and pepper
and served to the rats at a diner named PRAWNS DE JO;
that somebody feels beside herself with guilt about
and wheels her off to the sun-tanned arms of a specialist
and all she wants is for him to unpeel it off
and patch it up with a patch from the lawn of her leg,

18

but he's kitting her out with a rat-sized wig instead
that she keeps in a box
like pet pubic hair
she's secretly proud of because she is horrified by
but never wears because what's the use of a head
with a tuft of hair like a hat from a cracker on top
that's always about to come skew and slither off;
and what's the use of a scar if it's not to be mentioned,
and the milling of flies
and the sight of the flame-proof fireman
with a baby slung over his shoulder as if she's a pig?
And what's the use of the hand-knitted matinee jacket
the surgeon had to pick out with a pair of tweezers?

Mussels

What look like mussels
soaking in the sink

is a pair of soiled
electric-blue pyjamas.

Cashmere

Staring ahead like something biding its time
in a cashmere suit still smelling of marzipan

and the smell of the mushrooms her mother said smell of
         vanilla,
and tiny polished boots like hand-made beech-nuts,

he's waiting in the hall for her return —
if waiting is the word for not waiting,

for wanting her, and more than her, and breathing
very slowly, like an ear-drop.

Lips

She carries them discreetly
past the lodger

who crams them down her throat
like broken glass.

Egg

And when the lodger, on the second day,
asks her if she knows the word *cock*

she looks ahead and simply starts walking,
steadying the word like an egg.

Plums

Like drifts
of soft angora boleros

on little girls
who won't be girls for long,

the heavy plums'
faint dusting of white bloom

intensifies the blue
of their purple.

Vaseline

He climbs the stairs
towards the frosty thighs

thumbs and fingers itch
to prime with Vaseline.

Sheets

The sheets and towels of rented rooms
repeat

a million ways
of failing to say *home*.

Chicken

He's roasted her
a little gold chicken

whose crunchy breasts
he's skilfully removing

and laying on her plate
like roasted crocuses.

Jacket

Slide in the moonlight, arms, into his jacket.
Slide in the dark to the dark mahogany dawn.

Everything is possible. Just do it.
Imagine you're a tidal wave's first lawn.

Bedding

Their bodies hold
the darkness of his room

like bedding
in an empty caravan

where light comes in,
if light comes in at all,

as something matt
that's failed to be blue.

Bolero

Her doting aunt
knitted her a bolero –

a puff of powder-blue,
like thistle-down –

but what she really wanted was a wet suit
made of skintight lapis lazuli.

Everything

She's sitting on the steps in her nightdress
examining an ATLAS OF THE HEAVENS

in whose blue circles everything is possible
by virtue of the beauty of their names.

Roses

The circular blue
of the lodger's

inherited saucers
still burst

with their roses
as if there's no word for *dismay*.

Ultramarine

The china blue
of early afternoon,

being all there is to light,
accedes

to bands of dark
ferocious ultramarine

which nothing
can make waver from their task.

Larches

The garden is no place
for little girls.

Followed to the larches
by his shadow,

she's trying not to have to
hold his hand.

Baby

She wants him to never come down from staying up there
and she wants him to die
and she wants him to not be a man

and she wants him to look like and smell like
someone who loves her –
not someone

who's half not a man
but a baby
too sweet and too sickly to last.

Moon

You wouldn't believe
how still she can lie, like a moon

intent on the study of various kinds of smiling
and how effective they are as ways of suffering.

Stars

The night sky
carries stars between its teeth

like pins in the teeth of a woman
designing a habit.

Balaclava

Because she knows he likes her curly hair
she goes to bed

in a dampened balaclava
like some old ship

that's never going to make it
rocking itself to sleep inside a shed.

Snakes

The elastic jaws
of large disgruntled snakes

that lie in heaps
like soft exhausted mattresses

for whom she designs neat hats
and ingenious leashes

close over polished eggs
the size of sheep.

Sheep

In her dream she's in a greasy flood
and sees a sheep half-way up a tree

and when she waves
the lovely sheep shouts down

Get me a boat and a suitcase
and so she does.

Suitcase

Curls, to him, like weight, are irresistible.
She herself wants nothing more to do with them.

Better far to put them in a suitcase
and get a sheep to row them out to sea.

Cows

They teach her aunt, whose house it is, to moo.
They press against the window and the doors

and trample on the flowers and eat the lawn
and when she lies in bed on summer nights

they wander up the stairs and eat her hair,
and when the lodger comes, they eat marshmallows.

Bulls

Up in the room she watches the headless chickens from
and farmers like bulls shunting bulls into bays
and stuffing the heads of calves into clattering buckets,
by the single bed and the single peeling mirror,

up in the room big butterflies fall apart in
and windows stun the heads of tiny birds,
up in the room you can't hear the aunts and uncles from
calling you down for dinner it is so high –

having first removed her flame-retardant pyjamas
and said a last goodnight to the sky –
she dips her hair into the orange fire
she is old enough now to be trusted *never to light*.

Scarf

A small pyjama-case was all she wanted
but what she got was this enormous house

in which she's hunting for a scarf to wear
out of respect for the death of her late hair.

Home

When she thinks of home, the word *home*
echoes in her mouth

like *the dead*
echoes in the mouths of the living.

Doorway

The doorway where the night comes in in torrents
and keeps the yellow break of day at bay,

the doorway where she doesn't want to hear him from
calling her name as soon as she slips through the door,

doesn't want to feed the tiny face
entangled in her hair like a bat,

the doorway where she tiptoes in in stockings,
her six-inch kitten-heels in her hand,

she darkened once. It was her father's doorway.
He told her she must *never do it again*.

Terrace Gardens

The terrace gardens
where she used to play

have slipped into the sea,
leaving rock

up which a girl in ballet shoes
is climbing,

and slipping back,
and climbing forward again.

Boiled Sweets

He's on the landing sucking boiled sweets
that bleed their coloured syrups

into language
he doesn't know he doesn't understand.

Shimmering Lakes

Her every breath
is a silver hundreds-and-thousand

he crunches and rolls
till their tongues become shimmering lakes.

Sapphire

Sapphire light
is gathering in lozenges

and bouncing through the building
with the speed

of beads of glass
bouncing from an amulet

or rumours
of bright mountains coming loose.

Taffeta

It hasn't stopped raining for days and she's stiff with cold
and the prickly taffeta dress he is pinning her into
and walking her up and down and twirling her round in
sticks like ice against the skinny body
the lodger has himself designed the dress for –

as skinny as a deep-frozen rabbit
that didn't want a dress and wanted fur
and let itself be stripped and given sweets
and didn't want to thaw
and couldn't speak.

Milk

The neighbours and their elderly Retrievers
get used to seeing someone sitting there,

sometimes dressed in nothing but a nightie,
fiercely spooning milk from a tin.

Songbirds

Everything is much too big and fat.
His thumbs are buttocks

and his lips' fat red
is kissing her nipples

as if they were poor little songbirds
being kissed by a man with a plucking-machine for a head.

Shame

Shame,
like a white balloon,

still rolls its cry
from room to dusty room in search of flight.

Dawn

All she can do is be dumb like a baby night
that has no mouth and does not know what language is

and only knows one thing – it is essential
to get to be lighter than night and become dawn.

Wristwatch

She hears the little nights inside it tick
like starless nights in secret ammunition depots

where women in tight curlers on all fours
are falling over themselves to be forgiven.

Aunt Lou's Last Summer

Every afternoon they make her
fairy cakes

as warm and light
as little warm breasts

whose cherries
she can lie in bed and suck,

surrounded by a ring of old ladies
with sifted flour and sugar in their hair.

Help

She knew they'd never help her
if he hurt her

but when he does
she weakens and forgets.

Rain

With a head like a fish with something wrong with its head
and a face made of fins for raindrops the size of eyeballs
and frizzy hair beatified as waterfalls
streaming down her back like liquid fingers

she runs across the lawn and round the house
where aunts like boulders sink in plains of down
and thunder is a mother made of waterfalls
with water arms and water laps and kisses

drowning what he told her to, and forced her to, do, for him,
        with pain,
in driving rain:
rain is all she wants to feel touched by;
her only rule to spend the whole night running.

Running

The giant rabbit running through the woods
is running through the woods because of her —

because he knows the girl who can't stop running
is nicer than the one the aunts prefer.

River

Having left him alone in the house with that look in his eye
as if he were yearning again for a mother's arms
to come down and save him from what's going to happen next
that nobody else but him must even think about,

she runs like the wind to the rim of the swollen river
that's filling the fields and woods with luscious blue
and doesn't know how not to keep on telling her
nothing else remains now but to swim.

Blancmange

First of all everything goes thick.
Her hands and face are coated in thick glue.

And then she sinks; and then the word *blancmange*
fills the flooded woods with wobbly blue.

Angora

The soothing blob of wobbly blue
turns indigo

and calmly explodes
in tiny angora stars

where coloured pets
collapsing with a puff

are congratulating themselves
on dying happy.

Budgie

They offer her a bowl of warm Bemax
and wrap her in a blanket like a clock

and put her in a room with a budgie
and let her cry until the doctor comes.

Doctor

The doctor says
the lodger says I'm sorry.

But it isn't enough.
It isn't enough, I'm sorry.

How

How –
when she spent the entire summer playing leapfrog there
in her yellow shorts in the blazing sun
because she could get a good run-up
by starting at the apple tree
and flying past the famous Zephrin Druin until,
by mobilising all the precision and nobility
of the experiences of the great and wordless mystics
as she planted her palms on the plateaux of little friends' backs,
she finally landed practically waist-deep in water
because of the river that flowed along by the lawn
called to the presence of something that flew like joy,

of a flyer,
who, twenty years later and diagnosed sick,
by blistering the fingers of the blind
with cigarette-butts as they planned
their perfect suicide and suicides
and prising open the side-rooms' unopenable doors,
soon made new friends –
how could he insist on planting a cherry tree,
or getting her uncle's gardener to plant it for him,
the best and sweetest friend she ever had,
or had till then,
right there?

jamming her brain with cherries like boiled sweets,
her eyes with boiled sweets that couldn't cry
but blazed like stained-glass churches in the wilderness
till somebody's put her away
with the dead-end blind:

She shares a room with a milliner from the Valleys
whose twin has sprinkled quicklime in her eyes.
She doesn't even know what quicklime is.
You can hear her coming from all the way down from the
        side-rooms
because it is London,
the Sixties,
and she wears bells.

Mercy

The man she shows no mercy to is dumb.
At first he spoke odd words,
like angels coughing –
as if to speak would only hold him back –
and now, when it is obvious she is sick,
he doesn't even bother to do that.

Hairbrush

Anyone who touched her would be sorry
and that's why they've put her away, because they were sorry,
and they've put her away
where no one will see her but nurses
who, seeing her sit here alone with nothing to do,
are standing behind her
ceaselessly brushing her hair –
the most beautiful hair the lodger had ever seen,
the hair of angels,
lovers –

till she panics.
She cannot bear their need to understand her,
she cannot bear their need to get so close,
to fondle her scar
and take off their gloves and explore it
and climb up her hair
and drill through her brain to the sorrow
that never stops trying to snatch at the hands on the brush
as they ceaselessly, ceaselessly brush
her desirable hair.

Arm

Every week a different bored doctor
asks her how she is and gets no answer

and then an arm leads her back to bed
to sleep it off for a million years or more

and nobody comes and nobody mentions the lodger
until it is time for her little injection again.

Lobster

The Common Lobster
is morosely blue,

turning red when boiled –
in disgust

at being lifted
from her massive bed

where being blue
is how to reign supreme.

A Thousand Swifts

Perfect blue
seems to ask a question

but what the answer is
she doesn't know,

or how to ask,
or even if there is one;

and, if there isn't,
can there be an answer,

and can the answer be
a thousand swifts.

Galloping Alopecia

The lodger blamed the Galloping Alopecia
her aunt still nursed behind closed doors
on her;
and he didn't like the way she dropped her Ts
and he didn't like the skin on her heels
and the way she straightened her beautiful curly hair
and jumped on thistles
and didn't come home till bed-time
and came home covered in straw
and befriended dogs
with mud on her skirt and hands like gardening gloves
and the tone of her voice
and the way she said Can I get down
and the way she refused to sit down in his first-class carriage
and refused his sweets
and refused to look up from her beetles
and refused to decide to worship the ground he trod on;
he didn't like her knees like cardboard boxes,
he didn't like the way she'd disappear
as if she was right
and had a surprise for him
and she was the one who was never going to forget,
who witnessed his sorrow,
who witnessed his altered blood,
who came across him stooping in the bathroom
making up secret parcels of wild violets
for who or why nobody dares to wonder.
He chopped their little legs off at the ankles
and bandaged them up in damp cotton-wool.
He laid them out in rows like baby quails
with the backs of their poor little heads out cold on the slate.

Nothing

Because she is exhausted
and confused,

and doesn't want to argue,
and can't speak,

she dreams of nothing
for a thousand years,

or what the nurses cheerfully call
a week.

An Angel with Large Hands

She's looking for an angel with large hands
to take him in her arms
like perished silk

that isn't there,
like air is,
when you touch it;

to take him in her arms
like the evening
the moon discreetly takes from the sun.

Colonnades

Because the sun is much too hot for him
and she is strong and he is skin and bone,

she picks him up without a word and carries him
to somewhere cool the sick like him call home

where old men float down pearly colonnades
or spend whole days like fruit in tiled alcoves

doing without moving and in silence
what can't be done by floating with the living.

Motes

He died because of her.
She was too young.

She should have been attentive to the motes
that crossed his darkened rooms

as if in light;
she should have been attentive to his silence −

the fact that he was wrong
and she was right.

The Room

The room it was her privilege to come down alive from,
the rooms she ran upstairs to in the thunderstorm
to where it was impossible to come back down from
without a choir to guide her;
the room where she thought that what she'd found out was
that all she had to do was shut the door,
the room where the bed and the sweets and the door were all wrong;
the room in the house like a black plastic sack full of starlings
that smelled of sugared almonds and mahogany,
the room where somebody whispers to somebody else
something they don't understand
that doesn't bear thinking about;
the room where you follow the river
and seal the lips he climbs;
the room she wants to make absolutely sure of one thing about,
the room where it was like if you go for the door
he'll get you and chop your head off;
where this one thing is the only thing worth living for,
where this one thing's not even worth living for either,
this beautiful city behind the ruby door,
with all its shimmering supplicants and priestesses
and sweets the size of bedrooms
and bedrooms the size of beds,
and little girls in vests like frightened rabbits
too exhausted now to not be good,
is no more than a rabbit-coloured jelly
spiked with splinters of glass that no one sees,
and no one's going to see,
because it's over;
is no more than a deep-frozen household
enjoying the tranquillity of cold.

Sky

For sky that slips between her thighs like oysters,
for sheets like seas,
for laps like seals,
thank You.
Thank You for inventing space, O Lord.

Blue

By being awake she can wake to the sound of a trumpet
and a girl in Detroit makes bras from the bodies of lobsters

and how can a thousand swifts not shine like knives
and nothing he said or did could bring her closer

and now he's gone she does it all the time
and now he's gone her time is like an aeroplane

where any time you want her you can find her
making the most of the sky by discovering blue.

Poetry by Selima Hill

BOOKS

Saying Hello at the Station (Chatto & Windus, 1984)*
My Darling Camel (Chatto & Windus, 1988)*
The Accumulation of Small Acts of Kindness (Chatto & Windus, 1989)
A Little Book of Meat (Bloodaxe Books, 1993)
Trembling Hearts in the Bodies of Dogs: New & Selected Poems
    (Bloodaxe Books, 1994): includes work from titles asterisked above,
    the complete text of *The Accumulation of Small Acts of Kindness*,
    and a new collection, *Aeroplanes of the World*
Violet (Bloodaxe Books, 1997)
Bunny (Bloodaxe Books, 2001)

CASSETTE

The Poetry Quartets: 2 (The British Council/Bloodaxe Books, 1998)
    [with Fleur Adcock, Carol Ann Duffy & U.A. Fanthorpe]

CUMBRIA HERITAGE SERVICES
LIBRARIES

COUNTY COUNCIL

This book is due to be returned on or before the last date above. It
may be renewed by personal application, post or telephone, if not in
demand.

C.L.18